POPE LEO XIV

Produced for DK by WonderLab Group LLC
Jennifer Emmett, Erica Green, Kate Hale, *Founders*

Editor Maya Myers; **Photography Editor** Nicole DiMella; **Managing Editor** Rachel Houghton; **Designers** Project Design Company; **Researcher** Katie Cederborg; **Copy Editor** Lori Merritt; **Indexer** Connie Binder; **Proofreader** Susan K. Hom; **Series Reading Specialist** Dr. Jennifer Albro; **Expert Consultant** Joanne Maguire

First American Edition, 2026
Published in the United States by DK Publishing, a division of Penguin Random House LLC
1745 Broadway, 20th Floor, New York, NY 10019

26 27 28 29 10 9 8 7 6 5 4 3 2 1
001-357684-Feb/2026

Published in Great Britain by Dorling Kindersley Limited

HC ISBN: 979-8-2173-0607-7
PB ISBN: 979-8-2173-0606-0

DK books are available at special discounts when purchased in bulk for sales promotions, premiums, fund-raising, or educational use.
For details, contact:
DK Publishing Special Markets, 1745 Broadway, 20th Floor, New York, NY 10019
SpecialSales@dk.com

Printed and bound in China

Super Readers Lexile® levels 620L to 790L
Lexile® is the registered trademark of MetaMetrics, Inc. Copyright © 2025 MetaMetrics, Inc. All rights reserved.

The publisher would like to thank the following for their kind permission to reproduce their photographs:
(Key: a-above; b-below/bottom; c-centre; f-far; l-left; r-right; t-top)

Adobe Stock: Mistervlad 16-17, 20-21 (Background); **Alamy Stock Photo:** Abaca Press 42t, Abaca Press / Vatican Media 40b, 41tr, Archivio GBB 8b, DPA Picture Alliance 7, 21br, GL Archive 20tl, 21cla, Godong 26-27 (Background), ICP / Incamerastock 14br, Imago / Alberto Lingria 32cra, Independent Photo Agency Srl 13cl, Maria Grazia Picciarella 39br, Andrea Sabbadini 1, Vatican Media / Abaca Press 34, Vatican Media / Agenzia Sintesi / Fiorani Fabio / R.siciliani / Sintesi 12t, World History Archive 15; **Dreamstime.com:** Steve Allen 23br, Antoine Mekary 24, Meunierd 7clb, Palinchak 17br, Jozef Sedmak 18b, Xantana 24-25 (Background); **Getty Images:** AFP / Maria Grazia Picciarella 36-37, Anadolu 38-39, Corbis Historical / David Lees 36br, Vatican Pool - Corbis 28-29, Mondadori Portfolio 3, 12-13 (Background), Vatican Pool 27br, 44-45; **Getty Images / iStock:** Benedek 9tl, Sedmak 19cr; **The Metropolitan Museum of Art:** Rogers Fund, 1926 15tr; **Shutterstock.com:** Gabriela Carrara 26t, Marco Iacobucci Epp 30b, 32-33, 43c, Di Gregorio Giulio 35br, Godongphoto 11crb, MartiBstock 31tr, Simon Mayer 10-11, Alessia Pierdomenico 4-5, 22-23

Cover images: *Front:* **Getty Images:** Mondadori Portfolio; **Getty Images / iStock:** E+ / Jasonmooy (Background); *Back:* **Getty Images / iStock:** Alexey Yaremenko

www.dk.com

This book was made with Forest Stewardship Council™ certified paper – one small step in DK's commitment to a sustainable future.
Learn more at www.dk.com/uk/information/sustainability

POPE LEO XIV

Paige Towler

Contents

Who Is Pope Leo XIV?

Pope Leo XIV is the leader of the Roman Catholic Church. He makes decisions for the Church and leads important meetings. He offers guidance for the people who follow the Church. These people are called Catholics.

Pope Leo XIV is also the ruler of Vatican City, the smallest country in the world. It is located inside the city of Rome, Italy! This is where Pope Leo XIV lives and works. He works with special advisers who help him govern the Church. This governing group is known as the papacy.

Pope Leo XIV was elected pope on May 8, 2025. He became the world's first American pope and first Peruvian pope. Before him, many other popes led the Church during its nearly 2,000-year history.

Pope Leo XIV is the fourteenth pope to use the name Leo. XIV is fourteen in Roman numerals.

Roman Catholicism

Roman Catholicism is the largest and one of the oldest of the religion Christianity. Nearly 1.4 billion people follow this religion worldwide. It is based on the teachings of Jesus Christ. Roman Catholics believe Jesus was the son of their God. They believe in one God in three parts: the Father, the Son, and the Holy Spirit. This is called the Trinity. Roman Catholics follow the teachings of the Bible and the authority of the Church.

Before He Was Pope

Pope Leo XIV was not always the pope. In fact, he was not always called Leo! Pope Leo XIV was born as Robert Francis Prevost in Chicago, Illinois, in 1955. His parents, Louis Marius Prevost and Mildred Agnes Prevost, were of Spanish, French, Italian, and Louisiana Creole descent.

Mildred Prevost with her sons, left to right: Robert, Louis, and John

Creating Louisiana Creole

Louisiana Creole is a unique culture and heritage that carries a mix of traditions. In Louisiana, Creole culture developed among French colonists, enslaved and free Black Americans, and Indigenous Americans. These peoples' languages, food, music, and traditions combined to create a new culture known as Creole.

Robert and his family regularly attended their local Catholic Church. Robert and his brothers grew up listening to their mother singing in the choir. When he was old enough, Robert became an altar boy. Altar boys help their churches' spiritual leaders, called priests and deacons, during religious ceremonies.

Robert attended Villanova University, a Catholic university in Pennsylvania. He graduated with a degree in mathematics in 1977. But he soon returned to his true calling: his religious faith.

In 1977, Robert joined the Order of Saint Augustine. Over the next few years, he attended the Catholic Theological Union in Chicago. He studied theology, the study of religious faith and practice. After a few more years of study in Rome, Robert was ready to become a priest. Like all priests, he would be called Father.

As a priest, Father Prevost was committed to spreading the teachings of the Order of Saint Augustine. To do this, he moved to Peru to work as a missionary. Catholic missionaries seek to share the teachings of Catholicism far and wide. They hope to make life better for people in communities around the world.

Father Prevost worked for many years in both the US and Peru. In 2015, he was appointed the bishop of Chiclayo, Peru. Bishop Prevost became beloved by his community for helping to keep the region stable during difficult times. He also became a citizen of Peru as well as the US.

Chiclayo, Peru

Saint Augustine

The Order of Saint Augustine is a Catholic group that follows the teachings of Saint Augustine of Hippo. Saint Augustine was a bishop in the fifth century. Augustine's ideas were very influential in shaping Christianity. Augustinians believe in dedicating their lives to God. They promote charity and community.

Pope Francis meeting with Robert Prevost in 2023

In 2023, the pope at the time, Pope Francis, called Bishop Prevost to come live in Vatican City. Pope Francis made him an archbishop, the highest order of bishop. From Vatican City, Archbishop Prevost would help oversee the Church for all of Latin America. Later that year, Pope Francis gave him an even higher title: cardinal.

In 2025, Pope Francis died. The Church would need to choose a new pope. Did Cardinal Prevost have what it would take to become the next pope and lead the entire Roman Catholic Church? Some people thought so. But others did not. For one thing, no American had ever been pope. For another, Robert Prevost had not served in a high leadership position for very long.

College of Cardinals

Cardinals act as direct advisers to the pope. They help make decisions and govern the Catholic Church. There are around 250 cardinals around the world. Together, they are called the College of Cardinals. About half of them (all those under age eighty) vote for a new pope.

History of the Papacy

In April of 2025, the Catholic Church needed to elect a new leader. Whoever was chosen would take on an enormous job. Being pope is a huge responsibility. It means guiding the Catholic Church and all its followers. How did a big job like that come about?

The history of the papacy goes back to the founding of the Roman Catholic Church around 2,000 years ago. Catholics believe that Jesus Christ founded Christianity and the Catholic Church. Early popes were spiritual leaders who guided the Church. Unlike the popes of today, they did not govern any land or make local laws. This began to change in the Middle Ages.

An illustration showing the coronation of Pope Gregory XI

The First Pope

In Roman Catholic tradition, the first pope was Saint Peter. Saint Peter lived around 2,000 years ago. Peter was a follower of Jesus Christ. He helped spread the word of Jesus and helped lead Jesus's followers. He is considered a saint. A saint is a person recognized after their death by the Church for being holy. Catholics believe saints can help answer prayers and perform miracles.

A painting showing the coronation of Pope Pius II

Home in Rome

In Western Europe, the Middle Ages brought many changes. Many rulers and kings were competing for power. Invading armies threatened people across the land—including members of the Church.

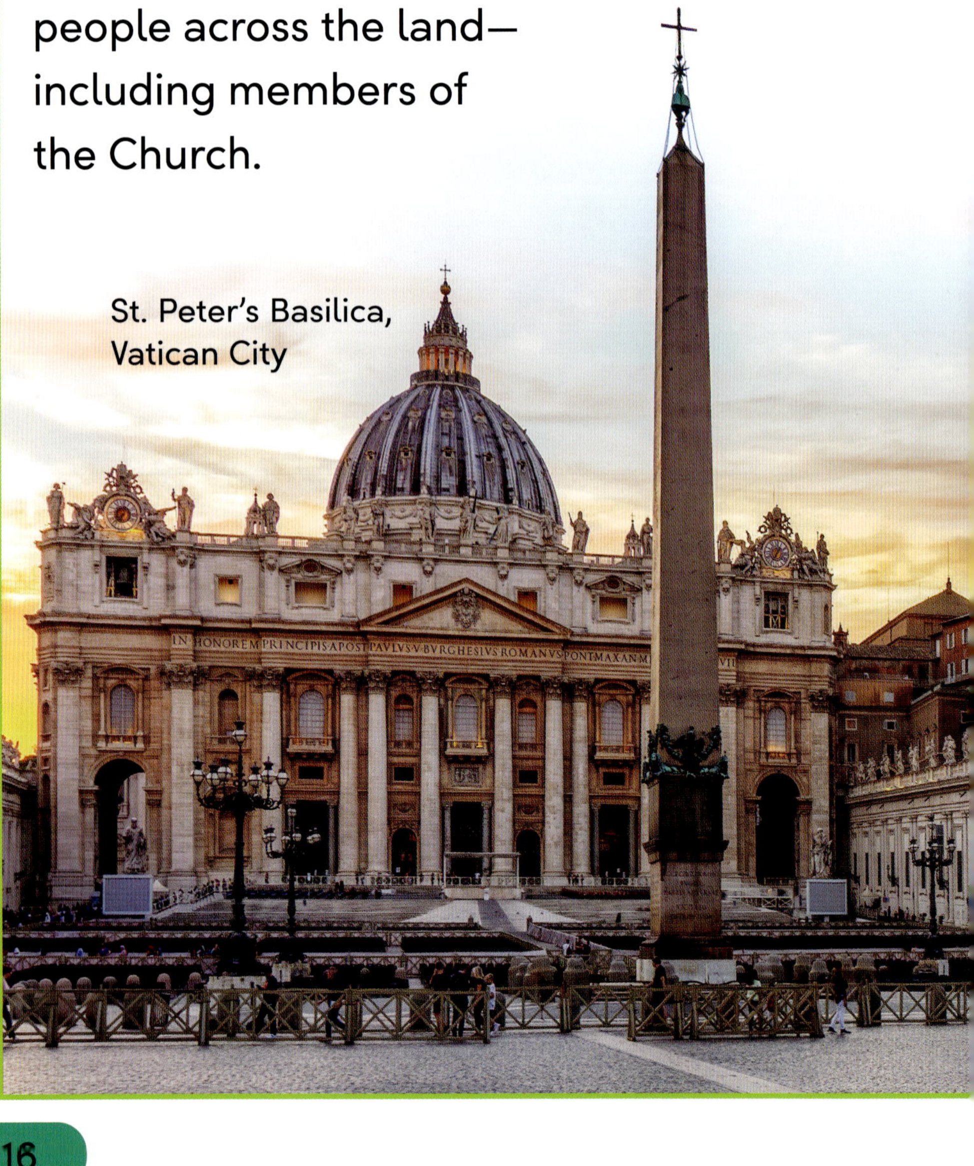

St. Peter's Basilica, Vatican City

In the eighth century, a king in what is now France decided to help protect the Church. He granted the pope some land in central Italy. This area became known as the Papal States. It became the pope's responsibility to govern the Papal States.

In 1870, Italy took control of the Papal States. Later, they made this area of Rome into Vatican City. The Papacy is still located in Vatican City today. The current pope lives in a building called Vatican Palace.

Vatican Palace

On Guard

Vatican City has its own military, known as the Swiss Guard. The Swiss Guard has been protecting the pope for more than 500 years. In 1506, Pope Julius II hired Swiss soldiers as his bodyguards. The Swiss soldiers were famous for their fighting skills. Today's Swiss Guard wear the same style of uniform they wore in the 16th century.

Notable Popes

Over the centuries, the role of the pope has grown and changed. The places where the pope has lived and worked have also changed. Lots of popes helped create these changes.

One was Pope Gregory I, also known as Saint Gregory the Great. While there were many popes before him, Pope Gregory I is considered one of the founders of the Papacy.

Pope Gregory I

Saint Gregory the Great became Pope in the year 590. During this time, many powers were competing in Europe. Pope Gregory I helped secure peace between foreign rulers and the Papacy. He kept the Church safe and independent. Pope Gregory I also focused on helping people. He made sure people had food and water. He also helped those affected by war. He is now considered a saint.

New Names

Today, it is tradition for the pope to choose a new name when he becomes Pope. This practice began in the sixth century but did not become popular until the 10th century. The new pope usually picks a name of a well-known Catholic figure. The name sends a message about their personal values.

Pope Julius II

Another famous pope in history was Pope Julius II. Pope Julius II helped make Vatican City what it is today. Julius II became pope in 1503, when the Papal States were in decline. He hired soldiers and made alliances that helped him restore this land. He is sometimes called "the warrior pope."

Pope Julius II also helped shape Vatican City through art. He commissioned a great church called St. Peter's Basilica. This remains the largest church in Europe. He also hired the famous Italian artist Michelangelo to create great works of art for Vatican City. One painting, *The Creation of Adam*, remains one of the most famous works of art in the world.

A Great Painting

Located inside Vatican Palace, the Sistine Chapel holds many great works of art. But the most famous of all is on the ceiling! *The Creation of Adam* shows the story of God creating the first man, Adam. The painting took Michelangelo sixteen days to finish.

"Being a cardinal is a mission of love with Christ, our Savior... a cardinal is called to give his whole life in service to the Church."

—Robert Prevost/Pope Leo XIV

The Papacy Today

Many popes over the centuries helped shape the papacy into what it is today. Modern popes are responsible for guiding members of the Catholic Church. They act as spiritual leaders. But they also do much more than that.

Over time, popes have become governing rulers and leaders, too. The pope governs Vatican City and the Catholic Church. He does this through a governing body known as the Holy See. A collection of groups called the Roman Curia helps the pope govern.

The pope also helps people around the world. The Papacy supports groups that offer people health care and education.

Symbols of the Papacy

The Papacy has several unique symbols. Each pope receives a special ring when he is named pope. Each pope also has a personal symbol called a coat of arms. And Vatican City has its own flag.

“A little bit of mercy makes the world less cold and more just.”

—Pope Francis

Pope Francis

The pope who came before Robert Prevost was Pope Francis. Pope Francis was elected pope in 2013. He quickly became beloved by many for his beliefs. Pope Francis believed that the Church should work hard to help people who experience poverty. He thought the Church should also help refugees. Refugees are people who have been forced to flee their homes because they are no longer safe. He also believed that the Church should help protect the planet and the environment.

Pope Francis worked hard to achieve his goals. He traveled the world to speak out and help people. Many people loved Pope Francis for his kindness and progressive views.

A memorial to Pope Francis

A New Pope

Just two years after Robert Prevost moved to Vatican City, Pope Francis became ill. He died on April 21, 2025. Many people around the world mourned Pope Francis. Thousands of people came to Vatican City to pray. More than 250,000 people attended the pope's funeral.

The cardinals mourned, too. When a pope dies, the cardinals enter a nine-day period of mourning. But after those nine days, they have a big job to do. They need to choose a new pope.

Who would the next pope be? Some thought it might be Robert Prevost. But others thought he was too new to Vatican City. The world would have to wait to find out.

"[Pope Francis had] a profound commitment to justice, charity, and mercy."

—Robert Prevost/ Pope Leo XIV

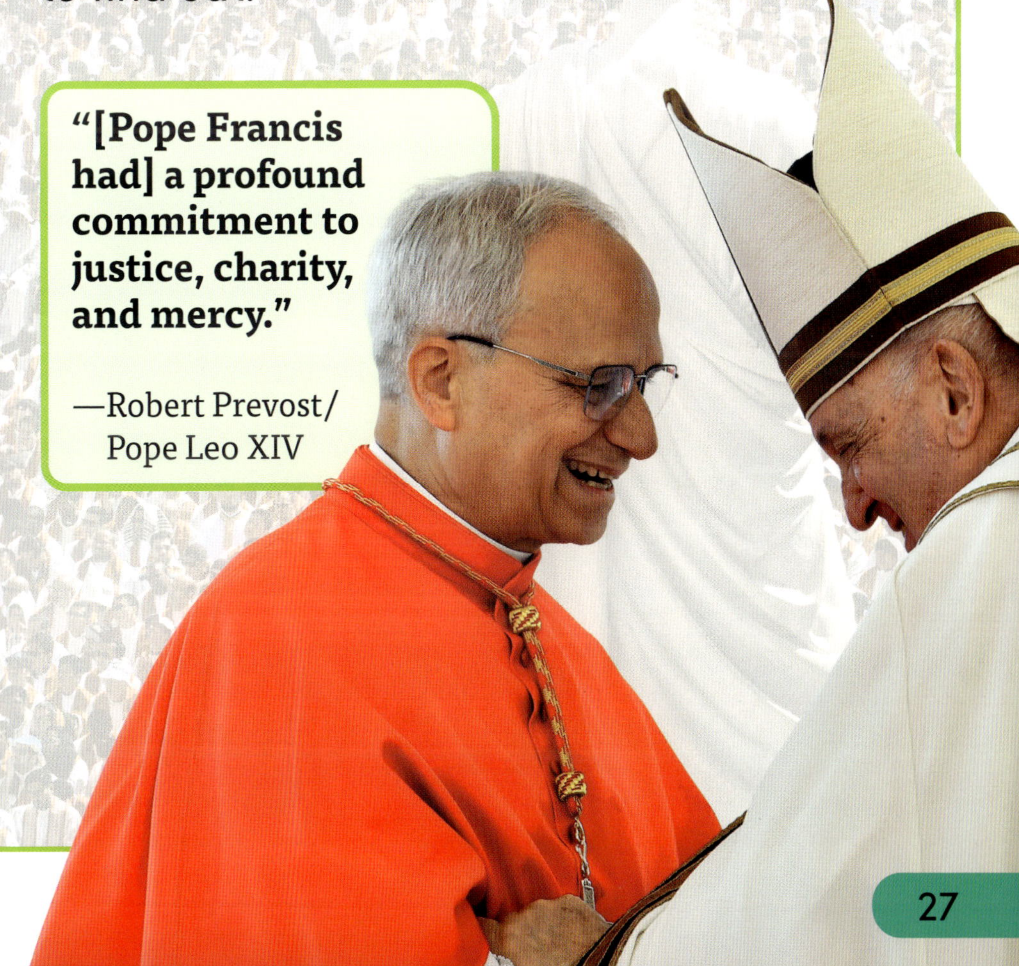

Choosing a Pope

Throughout history, popes have been elected by the College of Cardinals. This process sometimes takes a long time! In the 13th century, the Church created rules for a new election process called the papal conclave. During the papal conclave, cardinals gather to vote on who will be the new pope.

Cardinals in the Sistine Chapel

Centuries ago, the cardinals would all gather in one locked room. They were fed bread and water through a window. They were not allowed to leave until they had chosen a new pope! Today, the cardinals have more space: they gather in the Sistine Chapel. But they still are not allowed to leave Vatican City until the conclave is over.

Staying in the Conclave

Today, most conclaves do not last for more than three to five days. But in the past, they could be much longer. One conclave began in 1268 and lasted almost three years! The shortest, held in 1503, lasted just a few hours.

During the papal conclave, the cardinals meet in the Sistine Chapel. They vote on who will become the next pope. To be elected, a candidate must receive at least two-thirds of the votes. More than half the cardinals must vote for the same person. This can take several rounds of voting.

In Rome, people watching the cardinals gather for the papal conclave, May 7, 2025

Burning Ballots

Cardinals have burned their ballots during the papal conclave since at least the 1400s. This practice helped keep the votes secret once they had been counted. But the tradition of coloring the smoke did not come about until the 1900s.

Each cardinal writes his vote on a card called a ballot. Three cardinals are chosen to oversee the voting. They count the ballots. Then, they let the outside world know whether a new pope has been chosen. They do this by burning the ballots and adding chemicals to the smoke. The smoke leaves the Sistine Chapel through a chimney. If the smoke is black, no new pope has been elected yet. If the smoke is white, the cardinals have elected a new pope. Bells ring to help spread the news.

On May 7, 2025, the cardinals gathered in the Sistine Chapel for the papal conclave. There were 133 cardinals present to vote. Crowds gathered in the square outside, watching eagerly for any sign of smoke. The first day brought only black smoke.

Cardinal Red

During formal occasions like the papal conclave, cardinals wear bright red robes and hats. The red color symbolizes their devotion to the faith. The bright red birds known as cardinals are named after these robes!

On the second day, more black smoke appeared in the morning. But that afternoon it arrived—white smoke! Bells began to chime. An official announcement followed: "Habemus papam," or "We have a pope!" The cardinals had elected Robert Prevost as the new pope.

Priests in Rome celebrate the new pope

Pope Leo XIV celebrating a Holy Mass in the Sistine Chapel at the Vatican, May 9, 2025

Becoming Pope

Robert Prevost's election surprised many people. He was about to make history. First, Robert Prevost accepted the role of pope. Then, he chose his new name: Pope Leo XIV.

On May 18, Pope Leo XIV officially began, or inaugurated, his papacy. To do this, the new pope greeted and blessed the crowds in St. Peter's Square. Then, the ceremony began.

Choosing Leo

After he was elected pope, Robert Prevost chose the name Leo XIV. He did this in honor of Pope Leo XIII. Pope Leo XIII was a champion of justice and charity. Pope Leo XIV chose the name to show that he is committed to helping people. People think Pope Leo XIV may have important views similar to those of Pope Leo XIII.

LEONI XIII

For his inauguration, Pope Leo XIV held a religious ceremony called a Mass in St. Peter's Square. During the Mass, the pope spoke to his followers. He gave blessings. He was given important religious symbols. He received a special ring made of gold, called the Ring of the Fisherman. He was also given a piece of clothing called a pallium. This is a wool band that represents the pope's leadership.

Crowning the Pope

Today, the pope only receives the pallium and the Ring of the Fisherman. But for many centuries, each pope also received a crown called the papal tiara. This crown was made of three crowns stacked together. It was usually made from valuable materials like gold and gems.

Pope Leo XIV receiving the Ring of the Fisherman

Welcoming Pope Leo XIV

Pope Leo XIV was now the world's 267th pope! All around the world, people celebrated his inauguration. Pope Leo XIV had made history. He is the second-ever pope from the Americas, after Pope Francis.

He is the first-ever American and Peruvian pope. And he is the first pope from the Order of Saint Augustine.

People were excited to welcome Pope Leo XIV. Those in the US and in Peru were happy to have one of their citizens as pope. People in Chicago especially celebrated having a pope who was born in their city.

Now, it was time for Pope Leo XIV to get to work.

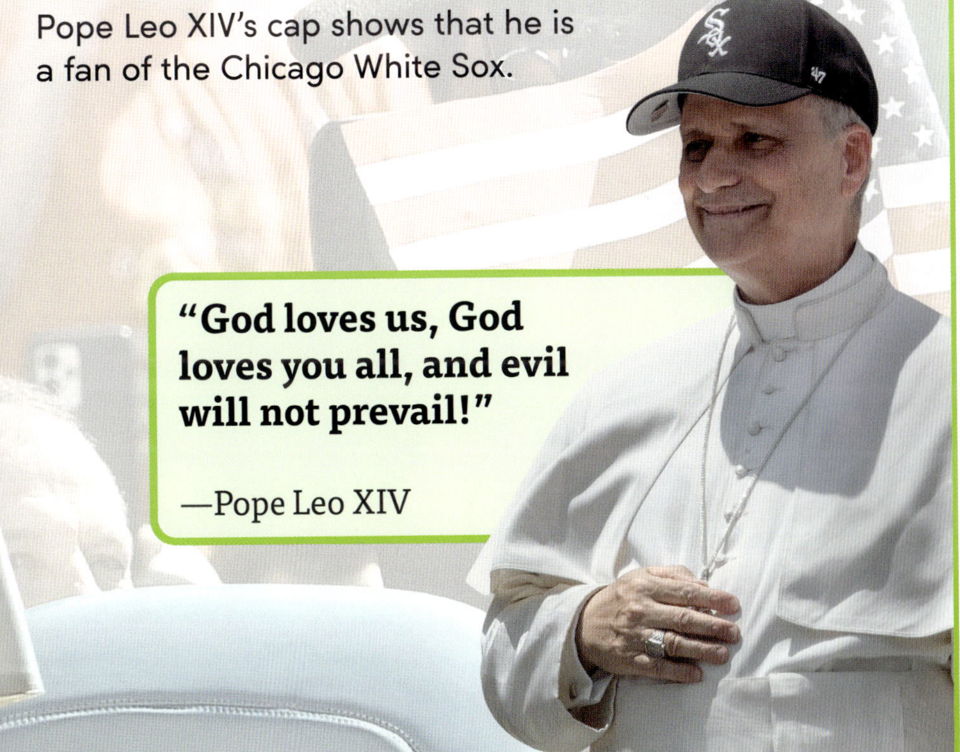

Pope Leo XIV's cap shows that he is a fan of the Chicago White Sox.

"God loves us, God loves you all, and evil will not prevail!"

—Pope Leo XIV

The Future of Pope Leo XIV

Like all popes, Pope Leo XIV has an important job to do. He must help guide members of the Church. He must govern the Church itself. Many people are excited and curious to see what Pope Leo XIV will do. His beliefs will guide his actions, which will help shape the Church.

Pope Leo XIV meeting with the Italian Bishops' Conference, June 17, 2025

> **"We have to be a church that works together to build bridges and to keep our arms open."**
>
> —Pope Leo XIV

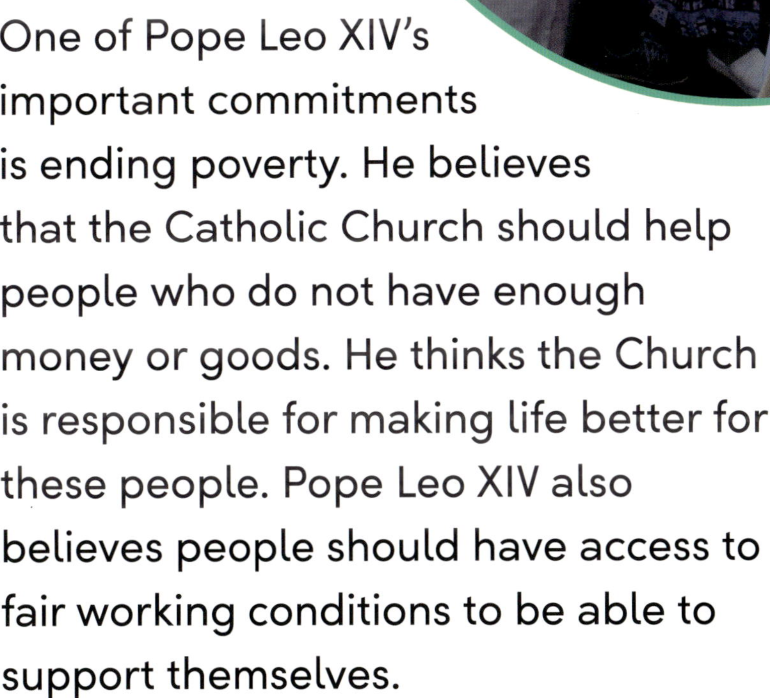

One of Pope Leo XIV's important commitments is ending poverty. He believes that the Catholic Church should help people who do not have enough money or goods. He thinks the Church is responsible for making life better for these people. Pope Leo XIV also believes people should have access to fair working conditions to be able to support themselves.

Pope Leo XIV is fluent in five languages. The card says, “Father Leo, man of peace, I love you” in Italian.

Pope Leo XIV also believes in helping people who are suffering in other ways. He has spoken out against war. He believes in working for peace. Pope Leo XIV is dedicated to helping those experiencing war and oppression.

Popes on the Move

The pope often travels to visit members of the public. Sometimes, he uses a vehicle called the popemobile. This special car has handrails and bulletproof glass. This lets the pope wave and speak to the crowds while staying safe.

Pope Leo XIV has spoken about protecting the rights of migrants. Migrants are people who move from one country to another. This includes refugees. Pope Leo XIV believes migrants must be treated with respect and care.

Pope Leo XIV is also committed to protecting the environment. He has spoken out about working to fight climate change, or the harmful impacts that human beings have on the environment. Some people expect that he will work to use energy-saving technology in Vatican City and encourage others to do the same.

People all over the world are watching Pope Leo XIV. They are excited to see what he will do next and how he will lead the Church.

> **"Our work is to enlarge the tent and to let everyone know they are welcome inside the Church."**
>
> —Pope Leo XIV

Planting a tree at the end of a Mass in Albano Laziale, Italy

Glossary

Ballot
A device used to cast votes

Bishop
A high-ranking church leader with significant responsibilities

Cardinal
A high-ranking Catholic leader who advises the pope

Charity
Help or goods given to those in need

Commission
To order or pay for the creation of something

Conclave
The assembly of Catholic cardinals to elect a pope

Govern
To control, lead, and direct

Holy
Considered sacred, worthy of devotion

Holy See
The central government of the Roman Catholic Church

Inaugurate
To formally begin

Mass
A religious ceremony in the Catholic Church

Migrant
A person who moves from one country to another

Missionary
A person sent on a religious mission

Papacy
The office and authority of the pope

Papal States
The territories ruled by the pope from 756 to 1870

Pope
The leader of the Roman Catholic Church and ruler of Vatican City

Poverty
Being extremely poor or not having money or goods

Priest
A Catholic leader who performs religious ceremonies and cares for his community

Refugee
A person who flees their home country to escape danger

Roman Curia
The group of people who help the pope govern

Theology
The study of religious faith, practice, and experience

Vatican City
A country within the city of Rome, Italy, ruled by the pope

Index

Quiz

Answer the questions to see what you have learned. Check your answers in the key below.

1. Where was Robert Prevost born?
2. In what country did Robert Prevost serve as bishop?
3. Who was pope before Pope Leo XIV?
4. Who elects the pope?
5. What year did Pope Leo XIV become pope?

1. Chicago, Illinois 2. Peru 3. Pope Francis 4. The College of Cardinals 5. 2025